D1278480

The Evolution of
Government &
Politics

The Evolution of Government and Politics in

GERMANY

GERMANY

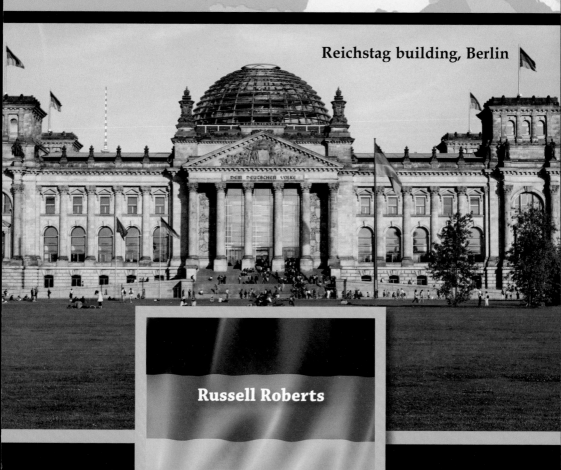

Reichstag building, Berlin

Russell Roberts

Mitchell Lane

Mitchell Lane
PUBLISHERS

The Evolution of
Government &
Politics

The Evolution of Government and Politics in

CHINA
EGYPT
FRANCE
GERMANY
GREECE
IRAQ
ITALY
NORTH AND SOUTH KOREA
THE UNITED KINGDOM
VENEZUELA

Copyright © 2015 by Mitchell Lane
Publishers

Printing 1 2 3 4 5 6 7 8 9

Library of Congress
Cataloging-in-Publication Data

Roberts, Russell, 1953–
 The evolution of government and politics in
Germany / by Russell Roberts.
     pages cm — (The evolution of
government and politics)
 Includes bibliographical references and
index.
 ISBN 978-1-61228-587-0 (library bound)
1. Germany—Politics and government—
Juvenile literature. I. Title.
 JN3221.R63 2015
 320.943—dc23
                                      2014008883

eBook ISBN: 9781612286242

                                      PBP

Contents

CHAPTER 1
Fiery End

The bombs slammed into the ground, shaking it like an earthquake and sending clouds of dirt and debris flying into the air. There was no let-up; bomb after bomb repeatedly struck the ground, released by squadrons of hundreds of airplanes flying overhead. People huddled in their shattered homes, hoping that the next bomb wouldn't land directly on top of them. Each blast made their homes shake, unleashing puffs of plaster and paint that choked the air like smoke.

This was Berlin, Germany, during the final months of World War II. The capital city of Germany was a bombed-out, desolate wasteland. Hundreds of buildings lay in ruins. The city was eerily quiet . . . except for the sound of the explosions. Otherwise the city was dead. There was no automobile traffic or pedestrians. Dead bodies littered the street. Those who could do so had long ago escaped. Berlin had once been a beautiful city. Not anymore.

The Germans were fighting the Allied military forces of the United States, Great Britain, the Soviet

Bombs falling during an American bombing raid over Germany in 1942. The airplane below the bomb has had part of its tail shot away and almost certainly will crash.

Union, and other countries in the bloody conflict called World War II. Now, in mid-April 1945, no more bombs were falling. Instead, a new horror awaited the citizens of Berlin. The massed forces of the Soviet Union were poised to attack. Millions of soldiers and thousands of cannons and tanks were about to wreak even more death and destruction on Berlin.

Huddled in an underground bunker amidst the rubble was Germany's leader Adolf Hitler. He was the head of the National Socialist German Workers' Party, or the Nazi Party as it was commonly known. He had begun the war in September 1939.

Initially German forces had been very successful. However, beginning in June 1941 with an ill-conceived invasion of the Soviet Union, the tide had begun to turn against Germany. Now the Allies were on the brink of defeating Hitler and Germany.

Yet even as it had been obvious for months that the war was lost, the German people refused to give up. "It's certainly unusual for a country to continue fighting to the point of complete self-destruction," said historian Ian Kershaw.[1]

Their world was being destroyed around them, but in some respects Germany's politics and government went on as if nothing was the matter. Until just a few months ago, applications for building permits were still being submitted and approved, as if the war would soon go away and rebuilding could begin.

The postal system provided an example of how Germans stubbornly made their government work despite the war. When trains couldn't run anymore because the rail network had been destroyed, motorcycles delivered the mail. When a lack of gasoline prevented motorcycles from running, the postal service switched to bicycles. When bicycles couldn't be used anymore, postal carriers walked great distances.

German government . . . functioning until the end.

How had it come to this? How had German politics and government contributed to their country being involved in such a destructive conflict?

Their choice for a leader was partly responsible. Hitler had cleverly used the dissatisfaction of the German people with the Treaty of Versailles that ended World War I to help him and his Nazi party rise to power. In the years immediately following the war, the political system in Germany had been the Weimar Republic, a democracy. However, Germany, which had been a

Adolf Hitler was born in Austria and grew up there.

As a youth, Hitler tried to enter an art school in Vienna, Austria, but was rejected twice.

unified country only since 1871, had little experience with democracy. Add to that the devastating effects of the worldwide economic depression that began in 1929, and the huge financial burden that the Allies forced Germany to assume for allegedly starting World War I, and the Weimar Republic was in trouble. It only took one political leader to take advantage of the unstable situation.

That was Hitler. He denounced the Treaty of Versailles and promised better days for Germany. This was music to the ears of Germans. In 1933, Hitler was elected chancellor of the country, second in power to Paul von Hindenburg, the country's aging and ineffectual president. When Hindenburg died the next year, the German people voted overwhelmingly to allow Hitler to combine the offices of president and chancellor. He called himself the Führer, meaning "leader," but in reality he was a dictator. Opposing political parties vanished, their leaders arrested and/ or killed. The Nazis were the undisputed masters of German politics and government. For the next 11 years Hitler ruled Germany with an iron fist.

Hitler built up Germany's armed forces—in defiance of the Treaty of Versailles—and in September 1939, he launched World War II by invading Poland. Less than six years later, with the Soviet army closing in, Hitler killed himself. Germany surrendered a few days later.

Hitler served in the German Army in World War I as a corporal. He was wounded and received a medal for bravery.

Adolf Hitler rides with German President Paul Von Hindenburg. When von Hindenburg died in 1934, Hitler became the most powerful political figure in Germany.

More than six million Germans had died in the war. Berlin was smashed to rubble; no more than one in four houses was fit to live in. Rats ran through the streets. Decomposing bodies lay under piles of debris. Police and fire protection were virtually non-existent. Other German cities were in a similar state.

Little did the German people know that the end of the war would bring more sweeping changes than ever before to the country's politics and government.

Once Hitler became leader of Germany he built a powerful military known as the Wehrmacht (Defense Force), in defiance of the Treaty of Versailles.

As Soviet troops closed in on Hitler's headquarters on April 29, 1945, he married his long-time girlfriend Eva Braun. The next day they committed suicide.

CHAPTER 2
Barbarians and Unicorns

The famous Roman statesman and general Julius Caesar conquered many countries and peoples. By 55 BCE (Before the Common Era), he had pushed Rome's boundaries to what he called Gaul. Gaul encompassed all of modern France and portions of other nations, including a part of today's Germany located west of the Rhine River.

Now Caesar was at the Rhine, poised to enter what the Romans called Germania. It was a country, Caesar said, inhabited by barbarians and covered by thick forests full of strange animals such as unicorns. The Roman historian Tacitus described Germania and its people in his *Treatise on the Situation, Manners and People of Germania*. "Who would leave," he wondered, "for Germany, with its wild country, its inclement skies, its sullen manners and aspect, unless indeed it were his home?"[1]

Tacitus added that Germans were extremely warlike. Tribes marching off to battle screamed war cries, and their women yelled chants as they urged their men forward to fight. Often those urgings

Julius Caesar's bridge across the Rhine was the first ever built across the river and demonstrated how Caesar and his army could go anywhere.

weren't necessary. As Tacitus noted, "If their native state sinks into the sloth of prolonged peace and repose, many of its noble youths voluntarily seek those tribes which are waging some war, both because inaction is odious to their race, and because they win renown more readily in the midst of peril, and cannot maintain a numerous following except by violence and war."[2]

Caesar felt it was important to "send a message." As he explained, "The Germans were all too ready to cross into Gaul, and I wanted them to have reasons of their own for anxiety when they realized that an army of the Roman people could and would cross the Rhine."[3] In a remarkable feat of engineering, his troops built a bridge across the Rhine in just 10 days. Thousands of

Roman soldiers poured across the river and headed east. But when Caesar learned that large numbers of Germans were massing to meet his army, he retreated. "I had accomplished all the objectives that had made me decide to take my army across the Rhine, primarily to intimidate the Germans,"[4] he wrote.

The Germans weren't really intimidated. In 9 CE (Common Era), Roman troops tried to move further east, well beyond the Rhine. German tribes under the leadership of Hermann (also known by his Latin name of Arminius) annihilated the entire force—about 20,000 men—in the Teutoburg Forest. Rome would never again try to conquer the Germans. Instead, the Romans established positions along the Rhine and the Danube Rivers. They moved no further into Germania, and German tribes could not launch attacks on Roman territory.

The Germans had no particular hatred of the Romans. In fact, sometimes during the following centuries when Roman troops were called home from the German frontier, Germans replaced them. This set up an unusual situation in which one group of barbarians was protecting Rome from other barbarians.

The Germans working for Rome were paid in land. They established several towns near the Rhine, such as Cologne, Augsburg, and Bonn, which copied the style of Roman towns. They contained temples, baths, and amphitheaters. The houses were decorated with fine artwork and heated with warm air.[5]

Larger, more powerful German tribes emerged, such as the Franks, Goths and Saxons. Meanwhile the Roman Empire was declining. The frontier defenses had more and more trouble keeping these powerful German tribes away. In the fourth and fifth centuries, those defenses often crumbled. The Franks and Saxons got closer and closer to Rome.

Meanwhile, Christianity had swept through the Roman Empire. The Goths and other tribes abandoned their pagan beliefs and adopted Christianity.

In 476, the last Roman emperor—Romulus Augustus—was forced by Germanic tribes invading Rome from the north to give up his throne. The Roman Empire was finished.

At about the same time, a Frankish king named Clovis began uniting the tribes in the former Roman Empire under what became known as the Merovingian Dynasty. In 751, King Pepin the Short replaced the Merovingians when he founded the Carolingian Dynasty. This process of unification reached its peak in the late 700s with the reign of Pepin's son Charlemagne, sometimes called the Father of Germany. He conquered and united the German tribes, such as the Saxons and Bavarians.[6] Charlemagne enjoyed German culture, and established his court in the German city of Aachen.

On Christmas Day 800, Charlemagne was crowned Holy Roman Emperor by Pope Leo III in Rome. This made him the Christian ruler of a vast empire that included Germany, France, Austria, and Switzerland as well as all or parts of other countries. However, it was an empire that was held together by the force of Charlemagne's personality. When he died in 814 his son, Louis the Pious, became emperor. Louis decided to divide the empire

Germanic general Odoacer forces Roman Emperor Romulus Augustus to give up his throne in 476.

No contemporary portraits of Charlemagne exist, so his appearance can only be guessed at from descriptions.

Clovis I united
the Frankish tribes.

among his sons. That led to a series of civil wars. The Treaty of Verdun in 843 ended the years of conflict and resulted in the division of the empire into three parts. As historian Steven Ozment notes, "With only small exaggeration the Treaty . . . has been called the 'birth certificate' of modern Europe."[7] The regions that would eventually form the two dominant European nations—Germany and France—became distinct from one another and developed separately.

Life was not easy for German peasants at this time. Most people lived in tiny huts in small villages surrounded by large forests. Life was hard and did not last long. A peasant could expect to live only about 30 years. People didn't go anywhere or do anything. They spent all their time trying to coax crops out of the soil, fending off Nature and the elements, and then dying young.[8]

An important turning point came in 911. "The east Carolingian line died out," notes historian Mary Fulbrook. "For some historians, the election of the first German king, Conrad I, Duke of Franconia, marks the real beginning of the history of 'Germany.'"[9]

While Conrad wasn't a very effective leader, it was a very different situation in 962 when the Saxon king Otto defeated a

Charlemagne enjoyed and admired learning and culture. He is credited with beginning the Carolingian Renaissance, a period in which art, music, and education prospered.

serious threat to Pope John XII. The grateful pope crowned Otto as Holy Roman Emperor, the same title as Charlemagne but which had fallen into disuse. "The coronation came to be seen as the founding of the Holy Roman Empire, an institution that lasted until 1806 and profoundly influenced the course of German history,"[10] according to the website German Culture.

However, Holy Roman emperors didn't rule over a united country. In fact, as Mary Fulbrook adds, "Germany is probably unique among modern European states in having a name derived not from a tribe or territory, but from a spoken language."[11]

Instead, the emperor was considered someone who could grant a prince and others a region to call their own kingdom. The practice contributed to the continued breakup of Germany into numerous small kingdoms, each with its own ruler. Other countries, such as England and France, were moving in the direction of a united country having one king who ruled over all. Germany, however, was moving in the opposite direction—lots of kings and lots of kingdoms.

Inevitably the presence of so many competing kingdoms resulted in warfare among themselves. This led to the rise of groups of merchants and businessmen who united to protect themselves and their business enterprises from the violence going on around them. The most powerful of these was the Hanseatic League, which was founded in the middle of the fourteenth century and included such German cities as Hamburg and Cologne. The league had its own troops protecting trade routes on land and sea, its own courts, treasury, and other functions of government. Another group was called the League of the Rhine, which consisted of numerous towns along the Rhine River. The rise of these powerful trade associations that functioned like

Some historians believe that Charlemagne's mother Bertrada was the inspiration for Mother Goose. Because of her large feet, she was nicknamed Queen Goosefoot.

When Otto III became the Holy Roman Emperor in 996, he made his cousin Pope Gregory V. Gregory was the first pope of German descent. Otto had to continually return to Rome to put down rebellions there. He was on his way there in 1002 when he suddenly died at age 21.

governments further contributed to the splintering of central authority in Germany.

By the early 1500s, Germany—or, as it was then officially called, The Holy Roman Empire of the German Nation—consisted of approximately 300 individual kingdoms, duchies, principalities, and self-governing cities. Austria, controlled by the Habsburg family, was the most powerful kingdom among them. They also controlled who was named king, or Holy Roman Emperor of Germany, though by now that was a fairly empty title with little authority or power.

On October 3, 1517, Martin Luther, a German monk, nailed a list of 95 statements challenging the Catholic Church to the door of a church in Wittenberg, Saxony. This was the beginning of the Protestant religious movement called the Reformation.

In Germany, which was heavily Catholic, the Reformation ignited years of religious warfare between Catholics and Protestants. In 1618 the rest of Western Europe was drawn into the savage conflict, which came to be called the Thirty Years' War. Unfortunately for the German people, most of the battles were fought on German soil and many Germans died. By the time the war ended in 1648 with the Treaty of Westphalia, thousands of towns and castles were destroyed or badly damaged. In some extreme cases starving people were reportedly reduced to cannibalism.

The Thirty Years' War was a critical event in the development of German politics and government, as well as that of Europe. The countries that had supported the Protestants became Protestant and the countries that had supported the Catholics became Catholic. However, neither the Catholics nor the Protestants gained the upper hand in Germany.

The Treaty of Westphalia had other consequences for Germany. Areas that had been considered part of Germany, such as the Netherlands and Switzerland, became their own countries. Yet despite these changes, Germany still remained a patchwork quilt of more than 300 independent states. What would happen next?

CHAPTER 3
Evolving

German politics and government had evolved differently than in other European countries. This evolution continued early in the 18th century, when the kingdom of Prussia—with its capital of Berlin—emerged in 1701. Under its most famous ruler, Frederick the Great, Prussia grew strong in the middle of the eighteenth century. German politics and government now became a struggle between Austria and Prussia.

In 1789, the French Revolution began. By the time it ended, Napoleon Bonaparte had become ruler of France. He began a series of military campaigns that conquered many German states, which were ill-equipped to battle the powerful French Army. In 1806, Napoleon forced Austrian Emperor Francis II to give up his title of Holy Roman Emperor. The empire that the French writer Voltaire said was "neither holy, nor Roman, nor an empire" was dissolved, and its role in German politics and government ended.

Under the leadership of Frederick the Great, Prussia rose to become a leader among the German states.

In its place Napoleon established the Confederation of the Rhine, which consisted of 16 German states and the Grand Duchy of Warsaw. This confederation lasted only until 1813 when Napoleon lost to Prussia at the Battle of Leipzig. Two years later, Napoleon's dreams of conquest ended for good when he was defeated in the Battle of Waterloo. Prussia played a key role, with its troops arriving at a crucial point in the battle and securing the victory.

There may have been another factor in Napoleon's defeat: Hermann, the long-ago victor at the Battle of Teutoburg. "Nationalists fashioned the Germanic leader into an icon to help them forge unity," wrote *Der Spiegel International* reporter David

The Battle of Leipzig was the largest battle fought in Europe until World War I, with half a million soldiers on both sides. Napoleon's defeat spelled the end of his plans for European domination.

Crossland. "Hermann, portrayed as a blond, muscle-bound warrior, featured in more than 50 operas and plays during the 18th and 19th centuries, such as 'The Battle of the Teutoburg Forest' written by German poet Heinrich von Kleist in 1808 as a call to arms against Napoleon's occupation. The figure came to epitomize the power of a young nation striving to be united and free. The cult of Hermann continued to grow during the 19th century."[1] A few people even went so far as to call the Battle of Teutoburg the birth of the German nation. A massive statue honoring him was erected near the battlefield in 1875 and today is one of Germany's most often-visited sites.

With the fall of Napoleon, that nation moved closer to coming into existence. The Congress of Vienna that met after the end of the Napoleonic Wars tried to craft a German country as a barrier

The statue of Hermann is 175 feet (53 meters) high. His upraised sword is 23 feet (7 meters) long.

against future French aggression. The delegates were also aware that the French Revolution had unleashed a powerful outcry in Germany for a unified state and constitutional government. They established the German Confederation. It was a union of 34 monarchies and four free cities under an Austrian president. However, there was no legal system and no executive or administrative functions. The ruling body was called the Bundestag, which met at Frankfurt. This was a group of 38 ambassadors, one from each country, with each essentially concerned with his own country. The most influential members were Austria and Prussia, and inevitably the smaller countries allied themselves with one or the other. The Congress of Vienna also gave Prussia more territory because it wanted to turn the kingdom into a major power situated between Russia and France.

German politics became a struggle between the Habsburg family, who controlled Austria, and the Hohenzollerns, who led Prussia. Neither family was in favor of a unified Germany unless they controlled it. Nor did they embrace democratic ideals—in fact, they were known as two of Europe's most repressive states. Even when revolution swept through Europe in 1848 and demands for democratic reforms were loud, both Austria and Prussia ignored them. German politics and government continued to exist in a stranglehold of repression.

The situation only got worse in 1862, when King Wilhelm I of Prussia appointed Otto von Bismarck as chancellor. Bismarck was no fan of democracy. He was, however, a fan of German unification, and he made no secret of the best way of achieving it. In a speech soon after taking office, he said, "It is not by speeches and majority resolutions that the great questions of the time are decided . . . but by iron and blood."[2] Over the next

Bismarck introduced the first national social insurance programs, including old-age pensions, universal medical care, and accident insurance.

several years, through deceit, trickery, and military action—his "iron and blood"—Bismarck gradually pulled together all the elements needed to form a united Germany with Prussia as the leader. Victories in short wars over Denmark (1864) and Austria (1866) were an important step, leading to the creation of the North German Confederation of 22 German states in 1867.

Bismarck wasn't done. He maneuvered France into declaring war against Prussia in 1870. The Prussian army crushed their opponents within a few months. The remaining German states joined the North German Federation to create the German Empire, also known as the Second Reich (The first Reich was the Holy Roman Empire). It was composed of 25 states, 12 duchies and principalities, 5 grand duchies, 4 kingdoms, 3 free cities, and two newly conquered French provinces—Alsace and Lorraine—with substantial German-speaking populations. Austria was not included, leaving Prussia free to dominate the new German Empire. The nominal leader was Wilhelm I, who was named *Kaiser* (meaning Caesar, or king). However, the real power lay with Bismarck. For the first time since the reign of Charlemagne, Germany was united.

Knowing that the French were bitter over the loss of the war and territory, Bismarck turned his attention to building alliances with other countries. In an effort to regain some of the power it had lost with its brief war with Prussia, Austria had joined with Hungary in 1867 to create the empire of Austria-Hungary. Six years later it joined Germany and Russia in the Three Emperors League. Though Russia soon withdrew, Austria-Hungary remained linked with Germany.

Otto von Bismarck

Bismarck survived an assassination attempt in 1866. He was shot five times but the wounds were superficial.

They created the Dual Alliance in 1879. This alliance would play a key role in the outbreak of World War I 35 years later.

Bismarck also oversaw the rise of Germany into an industrial power that rivaled Great Britain for supremacy in Europe (though both nations trailed the United States). However, in 1890 the new German Kaiser, Wilhelm II, fired Bismarck because he wanted to be in control. William began giving fiery speeches about German territorial aims that worried and angered other countries. In particular, he began a massive buildup of the German Navy which Great Britain, the unchallenged master of the world's oceans for many years, regarded as a direct threat.

Lasting less than one year, the Franco-Prussian War was a disastrous defeat for France. Prussian troops are shown entering Paris in March 1871.

Europe resembled a pressure cooker during the last years of the 19th century and the first ones of the 20th, with Germany seemingly preparing for war and other countries preparing to stop it. The pressure cooker exploded on June 28, 1914, when the heir to the throne of Austria-Hungary was assassinated by a Serbian nationalist. In the space of a few days about a month later, Austria-Hungary declared war on Serbia, Russia (Serbia's ally) declared war on Austria-Hungary, Germany (Austria-Hungary's ally) declared war on Russia, France (Russia's ally) declared war on Germany and Austria-Hungary, and Great Britain joined Russia and France. All Europe was at war.

The Great War (or World War I, as it came to be called) was at first viewed positively by many Germans, who anticipated another quick victory. Many German soldiers who went marching off to war that summer figured they'd be home by Christmas. They figured wrong.

By the time the Great War finally ground to a halt in November 1918, after more than four awful, bloody years, nearly two-thirds of Germany's 11 million troops had been killed, wounded, taken prisoner, or were missing. Kaiser Wilhelm gave up his throne and fled to the Netherlands, where he lived quietly until his death in 1941.

In Germany the Weimar Republic, named after the town in which its constitution was developed, was declared in 1919. It was a parliamentary republic, the first-ever for Germany. Unfortunately, the country had little experience in democratic government. The Weimar Republic's problems were compounded by the restrictive Versailles Treaty that ended World War I. The treaty was a disaster for Germany, which lost large pieces of territory, was deprived of its colonies, had its army limited to 100,000 soldiers, and was forbidden from uniting with Austria. On top of this, the treaty demanded that Germany pay 132 billion gold marks over five years as the cost for the war.[3]

No country could survive under such a crushing burden of debt. It unleashed runaway inflation that made Germany's currency virtually worthless and living conditions miserable for

The assassination of Archduke Franz Ferdinand in 1914 sparked the outbreak of World War I.

Germans (In mid-November 1923, one U.S. dollar was worth 6,600 billion marks.[4]). The global economic collapse that began in 1929 was the final nail in the coffin of the Weimar Republic. The political stage was set for a dictator to take control, and onto that stage walked Adolf Hitler and his Nazi Party.

By the time Hitler's ruinous reign was finished in April 1945, Germany had lost another world war and lay in smoking ruins. The victorious Allies divided Germany into four zones, occupied by the United States, France, Great Britain, and the Soviet Union. In 1949 the Soviet zone became the German Democratic Republic, commonly known as East Germany. In reality it was not a democracy at all, but a communist nation controlled by the Soviet Union. The three other zones also became a country in 1949—a democracy called the Federal Republic of Germany, or West Germany.

Broken into two separate countries, its economy in ruins, its people starving . . . how would Germany survive?

CHAPTER 4
The Modern State Emerges

A mere 20 years after the ruinous end of World War II, West Germany had become an economic powerhouse. Between 1950 and 1964, the country increased its Gross National Product by three times, its gold and currency reserves by more than 2,000 percent, and its exports by more than 500 percent.[1] Its industrial growth was twice that of the United States. Thanks to massive aid by the Allies, a quick rebuilding of its factories and industrial might, and the hard work of the workforce, West Germany was in far better economic shape than anyone slogging through the ruins of Berlin less than 20 years earlier could have imagined. East Germany's economy lagged far behind West Germany, but was also recovering.

However, they were still two very distinct countries politically: the communist East, and the democratic West. The West enjoyed freedom, while the East was repressive. Berlin was actually separated into East Berlin and West Berlin by the Berlin Wall, which was constructed in 1961. East

This photo of the Berlin Wall, which separated Berlin into two sections, was taken soon after its erection in 1961. The Brandenburg Gate, one of Berlin's most notable landmarks, lay in East Berlin (left side of the photo).

Berliners trying to escape by scrambling over the 12-foot (3.6 meter) wall were shot. The Wall served as a tangible symbol of the Cold War between the U.S. and its allies and the Soviet Union and its satellite countries, and dominated German politics and government during the 1960s, '70s and '80s.

However, in the autumn of 1989, the Soviet Union began instituting some reforms. Swiftly the communist grip on Eastern Europe—including East Germany—loosened. A trickle of East Germans trying to leave the nation to visit the west became a flood. On November 8 the dam burst: the East German government resigned. Two days later the leaders of the country, which was like a rapidly-deflating balloon thanks to so many people fleeing to the west, announced they would no longer try to stop them from leaving. The Berlin Wall "fell," in a manner of speaking.

Photos of Germans joyously climbing peacefully over a wall that they once would have been killed for trying to scale traveled all over the world.

Soon after this epic event, the two Germanys began exploring ways to reunite. On October 2, 1990, East and West Germany became a single nation for the first time in over 40 years. East Germany disappeared into the Federal Republic of Germany. Helmut Kohl became the chancellor of the newly unified country. Its president was Richard von Weizsäcker.

On March 15, 1991, the occupying powers gave up all territorial rights in Germany. The long German nightmare of Hitler and World War II was finally over. More importantly,

When the Berlin Wall "fell" in 1989, it led to the unification of East and West Germany into one country. West Berliners gather near Potsdamer Platz, one of the city's most important public squares.

Manufacturing, led by such companies as Volkswagen, has helped Germany's economy become strong. (Volkswagen means "people's car" in German.)

German politics and government were back in the hands of the German people.

Although German reunification had seemingly taken place quickly, the actual process was slow and sometimes painful. West Germany had been more prosperous than its eastern counterpart, and there were economic difficulties joining these two very different countries together. One measure was the Gross Domestic Product, which measures a country's economic strength. It had grown by a robust 2.3 percent a year between 1980 and 1991 for West Germany, but growth slowed to just 1.3 percent a year for a unified Germany between 1991 and 2000.[2]

Chancellor Helmut Kohl waves to the assembled crowd in October 1990, soon after Germany became reunited.

In addition, some people were concerned that a reunited Germany would one day rise as a major military power and again plunge the world into a world war, as it had done twice before in the 20th century. "We've beaten the Germans twice and now they're back,"[3] said Margaret Thatcher, Britain's prime minister.

However, showing how much German politics and government had changed in a half-century, Germany joined 11 other countries in signing the Maastricht Treaty in March 1992. This document established the European Union, an economic and monetary union in which the countries gave up some of their individualism—including the use of their own currency—to become members of a united European community. That Germany would sign the treaty sent a powerful signal that it was ready to be a member of a European family of nations, not a rogue country bent on world domination.

West Berliners sometimes used the Berlin Wall as a garbage dump, throwing their trash onto the other side.

Today, Germany is a democratic republic. It is the 14th most populous country in the world, with a population of over 82 million. The Federal Republic of Germany (*Bundesrepublik Deutschland*) as it is officially known, consists of 16 states known as the Länder (the singular is Land).

German Länder (States)
Baden-Württemberg
Bayern (Bavaria)
Berlin
Brandenburg
Bremen
Hamburg
Hessen (Hesse)
Mecklenburg-Vorpommern (Mecklenburg-Western Pomerania)
Niedersachsen (Lower Saxony)
Nordrhein-Westfalen (North Rhine-Westphalia)
Rheinland-Pfalz (Rhineland-Palatinate)
Saarland
Sachsen (Saxony)
Sachsen-Anhalt (Saxony-Anhalt)
Schleswig-Holstein
Thüringen (Thuringia)

The German constitution is called the Basic Law. It was developed after World War II, and is intended to ensure that no dictator can ever again gain power. Human rights and individual dignity are also important parts of the constitution. The Basic Law was initially adopted in West Germany in 1949. When Germany was unified with the inclusion of East Germans, the constitution was extended to them as well.

Before the Berlin Wall was demolished, enterprising Germans called *mauerspechte* (wall woodpeckers) chipped away small chunks and sold them as souvenirs.

Under the terms of the constitution, the German government has three branches: legislative, executive, and judicial.

The legislative branch consists of the Federal Parliament, or *Bundestag*, and the Federal Council, or *Bundesrat*. "The most important tasks performed by the Bundestag are the legislative process and the parliamentary scrutiny of the government and its work," according to the official Bundestag website. "The Members of the German Bundestag also decide on the federal budget and deployments of the Bundeswehr (Federal Armed Forces) outside Germany."[4] The Bundestag meets in the Reichstag in Berlin and contains a minimum of 598 members, who are elected for four-

Germany's Parliament meets to discuss some budgetary matters in 2014.

year terms by direct voting by the German people. However, a political party must win at least 5 percent of the national vote in order to be represented in the *Bundestag*.

The *Bundesrat* contains 69 members chosen by the Länder governments. Its primary function is to protect the interests of the Länder. Each Land has from three to six votes, depending upon its population. The members from each Land are required to vote together as a block, rather than individually. Since the members of the Bundesrat are not elected, its composition can change whenever one of the Länder holds an election.

The chief of state, or president, is the leader of the executive branch of the government. He/she is elected to a five-year term, and can be re-elected. The president is elected by a Federal Convention that includes all members of the Federal Parliament and an equal number of delegates elected by the state parliaments. However, unlike in the United States, the duties of the German president are primarily ceremonial. In March 2012, Joachim Gauck was elected president.

The most powerful German government official is the chancellor. The chancellor is elected for a term of four years by the Bundestag and can be re-elected repeatedly. The chancellor recommends the Cabinet ministers to the president. Angela Merkel was elected as chancellor in November 2005, and has been re-elected twice since then.

The judicial system is headed by the *Bundesverfassungsgericht*, the Federal Constitutional Court. It plays an important role in German politics and government, as its decisions have helped shape the roles of the Länder and the federal government. It has also defined numerous domestic and foreign issues,

Germany's national symbol is the golden eagle.

with rulings on such matters as abortion and the constitutionality of Germany's participation in EU organizations.[5]

While Germany contains numerous political parties, six are the primary ones. Most German governments are coalition governments; one party usually doesn't have enough elected members to pass laws without the help of at least one other party. The six political parties are the Christian Democratic Union (CDU), the Christian Social Union (CSU), the Free Democratic Party (FDP), the Social Democratic Party (SPD), Alliance'90/ The Greens, and the Left Party (*Die Linke*).

The CDU is one of two dominant parties in German politics. It is right-of-center, meaning it is more conservative than liberal. It sees the government's role as providing a framework for fair competition, low unemployment, and social welfare programs. It does not favor socialism or laissez-faire (a limited government role) in the economy.

The CSU is more of a state party from Bavaria, yet usually governs Germany with the CDU in a coalition known as The Union. Together, The Union makes up the largest political force in German politics. Although the CSU and CDU often govern together, they may clash on particular issues.

The FDP supports businesses. It advocates a free-market economy and individual liberty. It is sometimes criticized as being a party of the wealthy. In the 2013 national elections, the party failed to get 5 percent of the vote and therefore would have no seats in the Bundestag for the first time since its founding in 1948.

Germany's flag is made up of three horizontal bars of black, red, and gold. These colors can be traced back to the flags of the Holy Roman Empire, which included black eagles with red beaks and claws on a gold background.

Germany has become a staunch ally of the United States. US Secretary of State John Kerry and German Chancellor Angela Merkel share a pleasant moment in 2014.

Dating back to 1863, the SPD is Germany's oldest political party. It represents socialist values and is regarded as liberal in its outlook. It usually represents working-class citizens and gains much of its support from large cities where many workers live.

The Left Party (*Die Linke*) is considered more liberal than the SPD. Some people regard it as extremist.

Alliance '90/The Greens is a strongly pro-environmental party that favors sustainable development, such as wind- or solar-generated energy and ending nuclear power. Its members believe that humans bear the responsibility for climate change.

The German government's foreign policy has focused on enhancing and perpetuating its economic interests so that its economy remains strong. This is one reason why Germany has been so focused on solving the European debt crisis. The stronger European countries are, the more they purchase from Germany.

CHAPTER 5

Germany's Economy Ascendant

The German federal government plays a significant role in the country's economy through three separate government officers: the chancellor, the minister of economics, and the minister of finance. Usually these offices are not under the control of a single political party, but divided among two and sometimes even three parties. This means that economic policy is often a compromise among the various political philosophies of the parties/people involved. The decision as to which party/person gets what office is a part of the compromise that results from building a coalition government. Thus, depending upon which party occupies which office, official German economic policy can sometimes pursue objectives that are contradictory in nature and must be resolved by compromise.

Ever since Bismarck introduced the first old-age pensions in the 19th century, Germans have accepted a role for government in their lives, providing services such as pensions, health insurance, and unemployment benefits. The German economy is a social market one; it combines capitalism with the idea that society's members should be protected from economic and social need. This philosophy is called *Solidaritat* (solidarity). German tax rates are among the highest in the world. Its top income tax rate is 42 percent, and payments for unemployment insurance, nursing care, and pensions also come out of German workers' checks.

Yet this high tax rate has seemingly had little effect on the German economy. In 2011, the German economy had a Gross Domestic Product of $3.085 trillion. It was the world's fifth-largest, after the United States, China, Japan, and India.[1] It was the largest individual economy among all European nations.

In recent years, the country has needed all that economic muscle. Beginning in 2010, a worldwide economic recession hit some countries in Europe particularly hard. Greece, Ireland, Portugal, and Spain all suffered financial hardships that threatened

European Union heads of state and government pose for a family photo on October 24, 2013, during a European Council meeting at the EU headquarters in Brussels, Belgium.

Angela Merkel was initially trained as a physical chemist.

their economic stability. Germany stepped into the breach. By the beginning of 2013 Germany had contributed more than 220 billion euros (the currency of most countries of the European Union), or $280 billion, to those countries.[2] The money had been pledged through loans and financial support packages.

The financial rescues did not come without criticism of Germany. Led by Chancellor Merkel, German officials preached austerity and financial cuts for the affected countries, implying that it was that particular country's reckless spending that had led it down the path to financial difficulties. People in those countries resented what they saw as Germany trying to dictate and control their nation's financial affairs. There were protests and complaints against Germany.

Cyprus provides an example of this resentment. In mid-2012, it was teetering on the brink of financial instability. Germany once again led the way in negotiating a financial salvation package for the troubled country. As part of the package, Germany insisted that the country's banking sector be restructured. In response, mobs of Cypriots took to the streets. Some waved signs showing pictures of Merkel with a Hitler-like mustache above the slogan "Get out of our country."

Germany was experiencing "the reality of power," wrote the newspaper *Frankfurter Allgemeine Zeitung*. "Because Germany's economy is so strong and because the distance between it and its partners is growing, so is the jealousy."[3]

Angela Merkel is Germany's first female chancellor and one of the world's most powerful women.

In 2005 a monument to Holocaust victims was opened in Berlin. It is located very close to the site of the underground bunker which was Hitler's last refuge as Soviet troops closed in.

After centuries of disorganization, years of dictatorships, and decades of division, it seemed that Germany has finally mastered the ins and outs of being a republic in the early years of the 21st century. The country provides a model of a stable democracy, with regularly-scheduled elections that peacefully express the will of the people. Germany has become one of the globe's best citizens. The dictatorships that brought about both world wars are distant echoes that almost seem as if they belong to another reality. Indeed, Germany has not been shy about acknowledging its role in those wars, and keeps memorials throughout the country—such as a bombed-out Kaiser Wilhelm Memorial Church in Berlin—to remind its citizens of those dark days. Nor has the German government been shy about acknowledging its role in the Holocaust, the horrible campaign launched by Hitler and the Nazis that killed millions of innocent people in concentration camps.

No one can predict the future. However, with a strong democratic system that sends down deeper roots every day and an economy that is the envy of the world, Germany seems well-positioned to maintain its leading role among the nations of the world.

Kaiser Wilhelm Memorial Church in Berlin

Germany

——	International boundary
—·—·	State *(Land)* boundary
★	National capital
⊙	State *(Land)* capital
	Railroad
	Autobahn
	Other road

0   50   100 Kilometers
0   50   100 Miles

TIMELINE

55 BCE	Julius Caesar briefly crosses the Rhine River.
9 CE	German tribes under leadership of Hermann (Arminius in Latin) annihilate 20,000 Roman soldiers.
476	The Roman Empire falls.
481	Clovis I establishes the Merovingian Dynasty.
752	Pepin the Short founds the Carolingian Dynasty.
768	Charlemagne becomes Frankish king.
800	Charlemagne is crowned Holy Roman Emperor.
814	Charlemagne's empire breaks up.
843	Treaty of Verdun establishes approximate boundaries of modern Germany.
911	Conrad I of Franconia becomes first German king.
962	Coronation of Otto I marks start of the Holy Roman Empire.
1358	The Hanseatic League is founded.
1500s	Germany is composed of about 300 individual units.
1517	German monk Martin Luther begins the Reformation.
1648	Treaty of Westphalia ends Thirty Years' War, which devastated Germany.
1806	Napoleon abolishes Holy Roman Empire and establishes Confederation of the Rhine.
1815	German Confederation formed by Congress of Vienna.
1862	Otto von Bismarck becomes German chancellor.
1871	Bismarck creates the German Empire following military victory over France.
1888	Wilhelm II becomes German Kaiser, or leader.
1890	Wilhelm II dismisses Bismarck as German chancellor.
1914	Germany enters World War I.
1919	Weimar Republic declared.
1934	Adolf Hitler combines office of chancellor and president and becomes the *Führer* (leader).
1939	Germany begins World War II.
1945	Hitler commits suicide; war ends.
1949	Germany is broken into two countries: German Democratic Republic (East Germany) and Federal Republic of Germany (West Germany).
1990	East and West Germany reunited.
1992	Germany signs the Maastricht Treaty establishing the European Union.
2013	Angela Merkel is re-elected Chancellor of Germany and begins her third term in office.
2014	Germany observes several significant anniversaries: 100th anniversary of start of World War I, 75th anniversary of start of World War II, 25th anniversary of fall of the Berlin Wall.

CHAPTER NOTES

Chapter 1. Fiery End

1. "Ian Kershaw on the Last Days of the Third Reich: 'Hitler's Influence Was Fatal.'" *Der Spiegel*, November 18, 2011. http://www.spiegel.de/international/germany/ian-kershaw-on-the-last-days-of-the-third-reich-hitler-s-influence-was-fatal-a-798377.html

Chapter 2. Barbarians and Unicorns

1. Tacitus, *Germania*. Translated by A. J. Church and W. J. Brodribb. Medieval Sourcebook, Fordham University. http://www.fordham.edu/halsall/source/tacitus1.html
2. Ibid.
3. Julius Caesar, "The first Germanic expedition," *Caesar's War in Gaul* 4.16-18, translated by Anne and Peter Wiseman. http://www.livius.org/caa-can/caesar/caesar_t27.html
4. Ibid.
5. Andre Maurois, *An Illustrated History of Germany* (New York: The Viking Press, 1966), p. 14.
6. *Germany* (Amsterdam, the Netherlands: Time-Life Books, 1984), p. 73.
7. Steven Ozment, *A Mighty Fortress: A New History of the German People* (New York: HarperCollins, 2004), pp. 46–47.
8. Mary Fulbrook, *A Concise History of Germany* (Cambridge, United Kingdom: Cambridge University Press, 1990), p. 13.
9. Ibid., p. 12.
10. "Medieval Germany—The Saxon Dynasty, 919–1024." German Culture—Customs, Traditions, Language, History, Recipes, Etiquette, and More. http://germanculture.com.ua/library/history/bl_saxon.htm
11. Fulbrook, *Concise History of Germany*, p. 13.

Chapter 3. Evolving

1. David Crossland, "Battle of the Teutoburg Forest: Germany Recalls Myth That Created the Nation." *Der Spiegel International*, August 28, 2009. http://www.spiegel.de/international/germany/battle-of-the-teutoburg-forest-germany-recalls-myth-that-created-the-nation-a-644913.html
2. Excerpt from Bismarck's "Blood and Iron" Speech (1862), German History in Documents and Images. http://germanhistorydocs.ghi-dc.org/sub_document.cfm?document_id=250
3. *Germany*. (Amsterdam, the Netherlands: Time-Life Books, 1984), p. 87.
4. Ibid.

Chapter 4. The Modern State Emerges

1. *Germany*. (Amsterdam, the Netherlands: Time-Life Books, 1984), p. 95.
2. Simon Green and William E. Paterson, editors, *Governance in Contemporary Germany* (Cambridge, United Kingdom: Cambridge University Press, 2005), p. 9.
3. "Will Germany Now Take Center Stage?" *The Economist*, October 21, 2010. http://www.economist.com/node/17305755
4. "German Bundestag: Function and role," The Parliament of the Federal Republic of Germany. http://www.bundestag.de/htdocs_e/bundestag/function/index.html
5. Green and Paterson, *Governance in Contemporary Germany*, p. 2.

Chapter 5. Germany's Economy Ascendant

1. Kimberly Amadeo, "Germany's Economy." About.com. http://useconomy.about.com/od/worldeconomy/p/Germany.htm
2. Melissa Eddy, "Cypriots' Criticism of Bailout Rattles Nerves and Raises Ire in Germany." *The New York Times*, March 27, 2013. http://www.nytimes.com/2013/03/28/world/europe/germany-faces-criticism-in-cyprus-for-policies-on-bailout-program.html?_r=0
3. Ibid.

FURTHER READING

Books

Blashfield, Jean F. *Germany (Enchantment of the World)*. Danbury, CT: Children's Press, 2013.

Heuston, Kimberley. *Otto Von Bismarck: Iron Chancellor of Germany*. New York: Franklin Watts, 2010.

Manning, Jack. *Christmas In Germany*. North Mankato, MN: Capstone Press, 2013.

Miller, Gary. *The Rhine: Europe's River Highway*. New York: Crabtree Publishing Co., 2010.

Nelson, Robin. *Germany (Country Express)*. Minneapolis, MN: Lerner Classroom, 2011.

Tunnell, Michael O. *Candy Bombers. The Story of the Berlin Airlift's "Chocolate Pilot."* Watertown, MA: Charlesbridge, 2010.

On the Internet

"Federal Republic of Germany." Nationsonline.com
http://www.nationsonline.org/oneworld/germany.htm

German Missions in the United States
http://www.germany.info/

"Germany." Infoplease.com
http://www.infoplease.com/country/germany.html

"Germany." US Passports and International Travel.
http://travel.state.gov/content/passports/english/country/germany.html

Germany Travel Guide.
http://www.justgermany.org/

"Germany." Fact Monster.
http://www.factmonster.com/ipka/A0107568.html

Works Consulted

Amadeo, Kimberly. "Germany's Economy." About.com
http://useconomy.about.com/od/worldeconomy/p/Germany.htm

Crossland, David. "Battle of the Teutoburg Forest: Germany Recalls Myth That Created the Nation." *Der Spiegel International*, August 28, 2009. http://www.spiegel.de/international/germany/battle-of-the-teutoburg-forest-germany-recalls-myth-that-created-the-nation-a-644913.html

Eddy, Melissa. "Cypriots' Criticism of Bailout Rattles Nerves and Raises Ire in Germany." *The New York Times*, March 27, 2013. http://www.nytimes.com/2013/03/28/world/europe/germany-faces-criticism-in-cyprus-for-policies-on-bailout-program.html?_r=0

Fulbrook, Mary. *A Concise History of Germany*. Cambridge, United Kingdom: Cambridge University Press, 1990.

FURTHER READING

German Bundestag: Homepage. The Parliament of the Federal Republic of Germany. http://www.bundestag.de/htdocs_e/

German Culture—Customs, Traditions, Language, History, Recipes, Etiquette, and More. http://www.germanculture.com.ua/

German History in Documents and Images http://germanhistorydocs.ghi-dc.org/about.cfm

Germany. Amsterdam, the Netherlands: Time-Life Books, 1984.

"Germany." *The CIA World Factbook.* https://www.cia.gov/library/publications/the-world-factbook/geos/gm.html

Green, Simon and William E. Paterson, editors. *Governance in Contemporary Germany.* Cambridge, United Kingdom: Cambridge University Press, 2005.

Kershaw, Ian. "Ian Kershaw on the Last Days of the Third Reich: 'Hitler's Influence Was Fatal.'" *Spiegel International Online,* November 18, 2011. http://www.spiegel.de/international/germany/ian-kershaw-on-the-last-days-of-the-third-reich-hitler-s-influence-was-fatal-a-798377.html

Kitchen, Martin. *Germany.* New York: Cambridge University Press, 1996.

Maurois, Andre. *An Illustrated History of Germany.* New York: The Viking Press, 1966.

Ozment, Steven. *A Mighty Fortress: A New History of the German People.* New York: HarperCollins, 2004.

Schulze, Hagen. *Germany. A New History.* Cambridge, MA: Harvard University Press, 1998.

Solsten, Eric (editor). *Germany: A Country Study.* Washington, DC: GPO for the Library of Congress, 1995. http://countrystudies.us/germany/

"Where Do They Stand? A Quick Guide to Germany's Political Parties." *Spiegel International Online,* September 25, 2009. http://www.spiegel.de/international/germany/where-do-they-stand-a-quick-guide-to-germany-s-political-parties-a-651388.html

"Will Germany Now Take Center Stage?" *The Economist,* October 21, 2010. http://www.economist.com/node/17305755

GLOSSARY

ascendant (uh-SEN-duhnt) — Rising.

austerity (aw-STEHR-uh-tee) — A state of severely reduced spending.

barbarian (bahr-BAIR-ee-uhn) — A person in a savage, primitive state.

brink (BRINGK) — The edge.

chancellor (CHANSS-uh-luhr) — Highest government official in Germany and Austria; prime minister.

coalition (koh-uh-LISH-uhn) — A combination or alliance between people, factions, etc.

contradictory (kon-truh-DIK-tuh-ree) — Opposite.

currency (KUR-uhn-see) — Money.

deceit (dee-SEET) — Misleading; cheating.

desolate (DEH-suh-luht) — Barren, devastated, lonely.

enhance (en-HANSS) — Increase, intensify.

heir (AIR) — A person who inherits a title, rank, etc.

odious (OH-dee-uhss) — Strong dislike, distasteful.

parliamentary (pahr-luh-MEHN-tuh-ree) — Relating to a parliament, the legislative body of many governments.

perpetuate (per-PEH-choo-ate) — Make something continue indefinitely. to make last forever.

reign (RAYN) — Period of rule by a monarch.

repressive (ree-PREH-siv) — Limiting the freedom of an individual or a group of people.

restrictive (ree- STRIK-tiv) — Keeping within narrow limits.

sloth (SLAWTH) — Laziness, lack of effort.

virtuous (VUHR-choo-uhss) — Conforming to moral and ethical principles.

wasteland (WAYST-land) — An area that is barren or devastated.

INDEX

About the Author

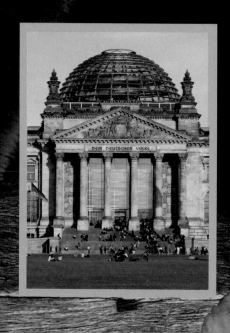

Russell Roberts has written and published nearly 50 books for adults and children, including *Larry Fitzgerald, The Building of the Panama Canal, The Cyclopes, Scott Joplin, The Battle of Waterloo,* and *Confucius.* He lives in Bordentown, New Jersey, with his family and a fat, fuzzy, and crafty calico cat named Rusti.